CRAVE

Also by Christine Gelineau

Remorseless Loyalty
Appetite for the Divine

Crave

Christine Gelineau

N Y Q Books™

The New York Quarterly Foundation, Inc.
New York, New York

NYQ Books™ is an imprint of The New York Quarterly Foundation, Inc.

The New York Quarterly Foundation, Inc.
P. O. Box 2015
Old Chelsea Station
New York, NY 10113

www.nyq.org

First Edition

Set in New Baskerville

Layout by Macaulay Glynn

Cover Photograph by Carien Schippers | www.imagequine.com

Author Photo by Stephen Herz

Library of Congress Control Number: 2016930015

ISBN: 978-1-63045-020-5

Crave

Acknowledgments

The author wishes to thank Neil Shepard, Nancy McKinley, Lee Upton, and Maria Mazziotti Gillan for their insight into and encouragement of this book. Thanks are also due to Raymond Hammond at NYQ Books; the community of writers at Wilkes University Low Residency MA/MFA Program and my colleagues at Binghamton University. As always, deepest gratitude to my family, especially Stephen, and to the dear friends whose support sustains me.

Grateful acknowledgment is made to the editors of the following journals and anthologies in which these poems first appeared, sometimes in a slightly different form:

"Sockanosset," *Pushcart Prize XXXVII* (2013); originally appeared in *The Paterson Literary Review;*
"Hard Evidence," "The Mare that You Loved" and "Pap Smear," *Prairie Schooner;*
"Distance," "Love Song," "Time is a Horse," "Jack" and "Curing," *Louisiana Literature;*
"Story" will appear in *Labor: The Working-Class Histories of the Americas;*
"Orbit" and "Christmas in Public Square," *North American Review;*
"Accident," *Broad Street;*
"What Men Do," "Physical" and "Fill," *The Paterson Literary Review;*
"Phone Call," *The New York Quarterly;*
"Scat," *Sentence: A Journal of Prose Poetics;*
"Trick Rider," "Method" (here titled "Backing a Colt for the First Time"), and "Hard Evidence," *Cadence of Hooves: A Celebration of Horses* (Yarrow Mountain Press);
"The Geometry of Grief," LIPS;
"Act as Object," *Ley Lines,* written and compiled by H.L. Hix (Wilfrid Laurier University Press, Canada). A line from this poem, "Act as Object," was included in Hix's poem "Wisps for Mortar, Traces for Bricks" in his collection *As Much As, If Not More Than* (Etruscan Press).

Contents

for Courtney & Jon,
Gregory & Lauren,
Jillian, Nathaniel, and Joaquin

Hard Evidence

Hard Evidence

For the most part people don't
want to be told the truth.

The woman who called us on Elka, the three year old,
said she wanted something quiet, something
she could learn on. That mare's been under saddle
just a couple months but she's a solid citizen.
It seemed worth the woman's time to look.

Before she and her husband even got the car
to a full stop, they'd gotten an eyeful
of Fyfe-n-Drum, the two-year-old colt
tearing up the paddock, tail flagged over his back,
nine hundred pounds
of gleaming testosterone on the hoof.

Oh, we got her on the young mare
and she slopped about in the saddle
as we'd pictured she would, Elka packing
her around placidly like the saint she is but
all the woman could think about
was that colt. The stallion.

Drummie was for sale alright but we could see
they were greener than fresh paint and would be
in trouble with him in no time so we told them
he wasn't for sale *to them.*
Some folks are hard to help.
After the "no" on the colt,
they left in a huff, gravel sizzling out
from under their tires as they pulled onto the road.

No more than a month went by and
we ran into them at an auction. She
kind of nodded at us and turned away
to study her catalog. After the hammer fell

on the last lot she made a point of coming up to me.
"Did you see the horse I bought?" she asked
in a tone that said, *guess that shows you.*

Which horse? I asked. *Sixty-seven.* Yes,
triumphant was the tone. Sixty-seven
was a two-year-old stallion, sired by a horse
more famous than our colt's daddy, bred by
a farm with a name more famous than our name
and she'd paid one quarter what we were asking
for our guy. Least that's how she was looking at it.

Showtime is a well-known sire, I agreed,
then slipped in, *Did you notice how
the handler had the chain shank run through
the colt's mouth to lead him?* The look on her face
told me she was an auctioneer's dream.
She'd been the opening bid. And the closing bid.
Other people there knew more about Showtime babies
than she did. Showtime babies could be gems.
Or they could be black holes.
Unpredictable, unstable, untrainable,
Wasn't anybody there looking to bid against her.
The auctioneer hadn't missed that chain through the mouth.
He dropped the hammer and cleared that colt
on out of the sale ring while the handler still had a hold of him.

Soft-bodied beings like us humans sometimes think
a thousand pound horse tipped with rock-hard hooves
is formidable-looking but in their own world
horses are known to predators as delectable herbivores,
granola-munching hippies in a fanged and taloned world.
For horses, the primary rule of survival is:
run first, ask questions later. It's useful
to understand this about horses if
you're going to style yourself as a horse trainer.

When that woman called us next
the one thing we could give her credit for
was that it had taken nerve to climb on
with her even-more-clueless husband
holding the bridle. Not much know-how,
but nerve. A horse that is being held
so he can't go forward, can't go back,
has one other option which not unexpectedly
their auction stallion opted to go for.
When he got to Hi, ho, Silver height
the unfamiliar weight of a rider on his back
threw off his balance so now he was in
a freefall in the direction of the weight,
up and over till he sprawled flat on his back,
with the woman beneath him.

This isn't the kind of incident you come out of
unscathed. Her good luck was that she did
come out of it, with a broken back, but she wasn't
dead and they got her to the hospital
without paralyzing her. It was her hospital bed
she was calling from to ask us,
Do you want to buy a horse?

Seems she and the husband had arrived at
the conclusion they weren't ready for a stallion.
My husband paused. Not to consider the purchase, of course,
but to bite down the phrase *I told you so.*
When it comes to the truth, some folks require
hard evidence, and she'd come by her evidence
about as hard as she could.

Sockanosset

My mother used to insist that living
next door to the penitentiary
and state reform schools was a good
thing, reasoning that escapees' first priority
would be distance between themselves
and the confines they'd left behind.
That's the story she would try to sell
us kids but we knew better, knew
about the boys who'd ducked from the shower line
at Sockanosset, slipped newborn and naked
out of sight of the guards, freedom
came that naturally to them.
When the clothes went missing
from a neighbor's line we realized the boys
were not cold, or suddenly shy but
crafty, looking to blend back in
with those of us who didn't yet appreciate
the true worth of one's own skin
and what it can cost to own it.

Pap Smear

They finally cornered him with test results
from the unsuspecting daughter's
pap smear. It's a vulnerable

feeling, lying on the narrow table
for examination, naked except
for the paper vest, open at the front
for easy access and the sheet that
is really a curtain: fit your feet
into the metal stirrups and spread
your legs, your own knees
stretch out that sheet between
your line of sight and the doctor
inspecting and probing your genitals.
The sheet is an adjective, modifying,
naming the event "procedural," "benign."

She was off at college. A Kansas girl, active
in her church back home and I imagine she's there
at the clinic to get her first prescription
for birth control, she and the boyfriend shyly,
responsibly edging to intercourse, now

the speculum tunnels into her,
the pipette swabbing her most intimate
chamber, the doctor, his nurse
cheery, professional, her paper
vest stained at the armpits with
sweat but then, it's over, legs clamped,
she's sitting up. Alone in the room,
wiping off the gel, getting dressed,
she thinks of Friday night
and the tender boyfriend.
It will be weeks before she learns
what the swab can prove, how police
compare epithelials from the walls

of her womb to the semen found
on the bound and strangled victims
of the serial killer, her father,
clinical proof of precisely
what is possible in this world.

What Men Do

The box was my idea.

That way if his hand shook
and, God forbid, he missed
the vital areas, her surge
of adrenalin couldn't propel her,
further maimed, into the dark woods.

Where do you place your hands
to lift a cat when her necrotized
organs are already flowering
from her in delicate folds? She
doesn't protest as I lift her
and settle her as gently as I'm able
on the newspaper lining.

While he aims, hesitates, she
waits. He shoots,
then again to be sure.

Apologists call it "the final kindness."
What men do when they live up
to what is owed.

During World War I
in Western Australia young
men enlisted along with their horses,
those brumbies the living element
of home that shared with them
every hardship, more intimate
than their own gun.

War's end the government refused
to let the horses back on the island.
They'd been exposed to African,
Asian pests and diseases unknown

in Australia and officials
were taking no chances.

That final night together,
the hardened young soldiers
gathered their horses for a race meet,
to drink in one last time that joy
in what their bodies could do.

Race over, they swiped and curried
the sweated necks, sleek flanks,
disentangled forelocks,
fed their darlings tobacco and fruits

then each laid his own pistol
in the hollow above his horse's eye
and squeezed.

Morning Prayers

for Jack Gerstle

On his way home from shul Jack held open
the door to his building for the tall black male
who was headed in behind him. Hovering more
than a foot taller, the paper would later
describe him as "hulking": was he on Jack
even before the elevator door slid home?

Jack carried a tallis, his cell phone, and about
forty dollars. What could the attacker have
been thinking at the moment his hand slipped
into the pants' pocket of the old man crumpled
on the scuffed linoleum? What could the limbic
mind have made of that intimacy, the feel
of that pouch full of human warmth?

But what is a pocketful of human heat
to hands that have already pummeled
an old man's face?

This is not an issue of race: the details reported
are only the facts the surveillance camera
presents. This is a question of how one could
be the kind of person shaped by his family's
escape from the Nazis yet still become a man
who hopes for the best in others, who holds
open the door for the guy he presumes to be
his neighbor, while the other becomes the kind
of man whose grievances are the gravid sun
of his own solar system, who sees others as props
in the drama of his own life, a man who picks out
the vulnerable, and with his own two hands,
takes everything he imagines he is owed.

A Secret History

1. Riding

She sits between them in the front seat, cinder of what connects them. It is the family's savage sabbath rite, the air an incense of shouting and the allure of blood ritual. The mother opens the door and pavement pulses past, insistent as any hunger. The mother leans out into the ferocious blur and the cosmos of the car wobbles as the father struggles to steer and to grasp. She sits between them, awe-hobbled, reaching nowhere: one small eye beneath the incendiary avenue of stars.

2. Music

She recognizes that throb at the base of the melody. Schooled as she is in caution, still there's the lovely lick of that light, the heat. The tremulous home no more than a sweatshirt she leaves behind. She remembers where she has left it. She has left it behind.

She is the fringed eye of a petal-plucked rose, the sepals furled back, opened. She feels the teeth of appetite and rides the music in.

3. Ocean

Sunshine, starlight, grasses, the fields of her childhood burning. Light slashing its fractured shards on the water. The drowning is rhythmic, slick. She can slide into and out of herself, nipples alert as little animals, the future a beacon, a lighthouse always out of reach. A contrail of silver bubbles rises. Arcing into the undertow she thinks: one treasure is as good as another to the sea.

Physical

One more form the graduate school
required you to fill out so I thumbed
through the phone book and picked out a name
of some doctor near campus.

"Shocking to lose a mother so young–
to pneumonia– in a hospital– in the middle
of Connecticut—late in the twentieth century."
He'd picked the information off the medical history
I'd been required to fill out of course but
what shocked me was how he purred
the seemingly solicitous words
        while his eyes
     his hands   said   smooth
     delicious   pert
   there in your tissue paper vest

      My skin
    crackled like electricity
snapping no no no no no

He backed off suavely   had I imagined?
     no no no

These many decades later, age has its way.
Opportunities increase to visit new doctors
and expose your vulnerabilities to them
and I know myself clearly now
to be part of the assembly line of lumpen
flesh in need, the crepe and folds of which
the gloved physicians professionally probe,
all the unfit, un-airbrushed, unlovely
mounds of us and I think of that long ago
doctor and my long ago young body
and I do not forgive him.
Not one bit.

Phone call

He rang close to eleven and he called me
by name though my first name has not been
listed in the book for more than twenty years.
Just past my reflection on the dark window glass
branches worried the screen, a soft rasping.

Christine, it's John. No John I recognized.
John who? He called me by name once more
and hung up. The pool of pale
light in the room prickled.

Star, six, nine, and the cool voice
with the innocuous numbers.

The Internet identifies only
a cell phone from a nearby town.

Are you in bed, Chris? The phone calls
all those years ago that prompted me
to list with just a first initial. I *was*
in bed each time he called
in my isolated farm house, high
up on the hill, odd moments of the day
whenever my newborn son would sleep.
How could he know this so unfailingly?
What did he want?

At police academy graduation this spring that
same son won Top Gun award, a moment of
exquisite irony for the mother who wouldn't
let him have even a squirt gun for a toy. Now
my son asks me for the number and can't wait
to give the guy a call.

Hey, John! *Hey, how ya doing,* John asks at first,
then, *who is this?* Now it's John who's wondering
How did he get my number?
What does he want?
What does he know?

Fill

At the evaporating funeral, the one where the memory
of the deceased evanesced as fast as the rabbi's words
faded, no one there knew the deceased, not even
the son the rest of us were there to support.

The son and five of his friends carried the coffin,
we three women followed in appropriately decorous
measure. If one counted the rabbi, and the rabbi agreed
to count the women, we could just be a minyan.

The sweating rabbi was trying harder than anyone
and even he was racing through prayers as those
used to davening do, pausing once to turn off
his cell phone when it embarrassed him by ringing.

Because he did not know her, the good qualities
the rabbi struggled to invent for her for his eulogy,
pieced from the tiny scraps the son had offered the day before,
were kinder than the truths the rabbi did not know.

When the rabbi hopefully asked the son if he
would like to say a few words, Fred shook his head,
"no." Silence was the kindest, the most honest thing
he could think to say on her behalf, that mother

who had ceased to be his mother all those decades ago
when his young sister failed to make it home from the hospital,
a sudden victim of childhood onset diabetes, a shock
from which the family never righted itself.

Once more today, we gathered did what we could
to shovel dirt into the yawning hole that first loss blasted.

On their way to the grave the rabbi had the pallbearers
pause seven times, and later had the mourners flick
their first three shovelfuls of soil onto the coffin
with the spade reversed, to show our reluctance, he said,

but we were not reluctant, we were eager there in the summer
morning sun to grab those spades and throw the cool earth down,
to blot out the unrecoverable, and wipe the soil from our hands
as we headed, lightened, back to our cars.

Accident

I too have confused what was just
beginning with what had already reached
its end.

Why should you acknowledge the innocence
of trees, the patience that looks now to your
family

like waiting, menace even, but is only these trees'
unthought unfolding? Here between the sinuous
bellow

of the river bend and the road that loops beside it,
has looped beside it all the years of your life, well
before

your life began, the persistent serenity of oak, maple,
pine does not anticipate what they have no capacity
to resist:

you flown free from the crumbling carapace of what had
been your car, released finally into those trees' irrevocable
embrace.

Daylilies Make Us Mindful :

that long nipple
      of a bud
unfurls

    to a supple
flute,
      the opened

flare of its all-day
      welcome, winged
        suitors deep

in the petalled throat
   of summer :
     how not to

feel now the spent grace
     of our own days :
   when few enough

      remain to sense
the singular cool
    of evening's approach.

Paterson, N.J.

is a woman, not young, not
glamorous, in the black dress that makes her
look sturdy but tidy, respectable, that
black dress, and sensible
shoes; she is running now
in those shoes though ordinarily
she does not even walk easily, but now
she smells the risk in the footsteps
behind her and she concedes
nothing, makes no pretense
of ladylike behavior or dissembling
politeness, no, she sprints
with her bundles and her pocketbook,
her keys bristling in her hand:
by the time the punk catches up
enough for her to see the knife, her car door
has slammed already and
she is leaning into the horn
and stabbing the key in the ignition
like there is no tomorrow
unless she makes it
with her own two hands.

for Maria Mazziotti Gillan

Christmas in Public Square

The electronic bird calls of the blind
crossing signals carol the Christmas tree
guy-wired to the hardwoods in the center
of Center City: a misshapen dowager
of a spruce bespangled in rumpled rows
of colored lights, her tiara star askew.
In her heyday Wilkes-Barre had been
the Diamond City, black diamonds
of anthracite coal.   Over time oil and gas
siphoned off much of coal's kingdom
but it was the Knox Mine disaster
of 1959 that sealed things.

Are we surprised to hear how old
the story is, how often we repeat ourselves?
Mine officials sent the miners down to burrow
illegally beneath the Susquehanna.
When the riverbed caved in it took three days
of jamming railroad cars, culm, whatever debris
came to hand into the voracious whirlpool that opened
before the wound could be staunched but by then
twelve miners, and the fortunes of Wilkes-Barre,
had been swept into the web of mines now irrevocably
plugged by ten billion gallons of river water.

O Shepherds, o silent night, beneath this tree,
in the hollowed-out heart of one more
once-prosperous American city, as evening
settles into night, a lone policeman
in his idling patrol car watches
wreathed in silvery exhaust.

Sewol Triptych

1.

The sea moans its gray refrain against
the toppled ferry's submerged hull while
the slick-suited divers roll backwards
off the lips of the rescue boats then
will their limbs to propel them
into the dark-chambered heart
where the dead children wait.

2.

To the extent we can understand them
to have acted on thought and not instinct alone,
surely the captain and crew who instructed
those children to stay below decks, while they
themselves left the world turning over on itself,
gave themselves to the water's cold clasp, surely
then they were picturing some chance of another
plane on which something might occur
which would better approximate living than what
the remains of their lives actually ever will.

3.

Parents gather in the makeshift space of an
auditorium on Jindo Island, waiting for the white
boards to display small identifying details
of the latest bodies brought to shore : female,
braces, hoodie, track pants, red nail polish. Not listed :
the finger bones broken in the desperation of last moments.

The parents are both numbed, and attenuated
to one another, cohered in an animal synchronicity :
the world peering in over news cameras needs
no one to translate for them : their cries
beyond language : sharp shafts of sound.

Story

1.

It was the story she told
relentlessly
while he was still in the hospital:
repeated like a lesson
her future depended upon.

And then it became
the story she no longer told,
the story that lived
alone in the dark.

2.

His arms caught fire.
That's how he was rescued:
the thin plume of smoke
from the burning arms
of the conscious man trapped
in the hay baler attracted the notice
of a man driving by
the isolated hay field.

The man with his arms
snared in the mangle
of the baler gave directions
for his own rescue: how to kill
the power on the PTO, and when
the ambulance arrived, how to
release him into
the remainder of his life.

3.

Heading into the operating room
the surgeon told the wife
he could not save the right arm
but there might be
hope for the left.

It was hours
in the waiting room before the nurse
appeared and asked, "Mrs. Herz?"

then wordlessly
handed her his wedding ring.

Crave

———————————————————————————

Orbit

This poem tilts its chair back at precarious angles. This poem has committed its lines to memory, it cartwheels and backbends before it gets in the car, this poem eats at the heart of America, it has a hearty appetite for golden waves and fetid rhetoric, this poem licks down dreams for dessert, cleanses them like a mother cat, this poem is a good sport. It plays air guitar like an avenging angel, when first conceived this poem has verbs hot enough to broil a sausage on, even cooled it is too saucy for the gander. This poem has wanderlust in its genes, though it would prefer to be in sweats, and a red hat, this poem will not be confined, or confused into owning a labradoodle, this poem has its faith in instinctual designs, it piles up like late season snow and melts into raucous rivulets, a silver sorcery of peppy anthems, this poem has the jaws of a pit bull and cannon bones of steel, it gallops from one genre to the next without ever resorting to the whip, it cycles past the Whimsey Poplars humming popular whimsies. This poem is really getting somewhere. It shakes baubles and lightning strikes from its hair, downs the glass of brandied plutonium, throws back its head, and sings.

Scat

Coyote leaves its scat like a phone number in a public restroom. Doberman is salivating to answer the call. Sure, he's heard the Trickster stories but what can you tell a Doberman? He's on a quest, *the* quest, and the scent is fine as he gambols through the dappled forest, dreaming his delights. Who is there really to blame when the pack jumps him just for sport? Who's to say he won't always treasure his scars, the lackadaisical tilt to his torn ear, the memory of sweet shriek and snarl among the trees?

Distance

Vermeer's Lady Writing a Letter

His Model:

He looks at me as directly as God
looked upon the earth as He created it.
That gaze kindles me, a fervor like the flickering
of this silk robe he has wrapped me in.
Light pours in over the high shutter,
a golden luster I sit drenched in,
pretending I could write the letter
waiting here before me. He asks only
that I hold the quill and gaze trembling
back at him, exactly as the small trapped beast
of my heart hungers for me to do.

Vermeer:

The eye is a foolish thing, emotional,
happy to be gulled. My faith is in color,
and the opulence of light. Observe
this mantle's fabric: the eye sees
the brightness the darkness makes it
desire but pigment must keep faith
with shape and glint: orpiment ignites
the glow off the shoulder, lights
her face, while cadmium, lemon, naples,
aureolin, ochre, umber, citron and
undertones of burnt sienna ripple and pucker
the silk with imperturbable fidelity.

His Model:

It is wearisome to sit so quietly
motionless as a nun at her prayers.
By now the arc of my back prickles
from stasis and the quill cramps in my hand.
One decorative tack from the edge of the chair's

leather padding bites into my leg through the kirtle
and petticoats. Still, all will be forgotten
when I see his ardent watching of me
transformed to canvas, the brush in his hand
rendering permanent my smooth brow,
small smile, and my eyes openly looking back at him.

Vermeer:

I was a pupil first to tulips, each petal
a learned lecturer on luminosity's
plushness. I devoured every lesson offered
by the blush, the sheen. I learned to trust
what has no need even to acknowledge me.
Now, I subsist on the insubstantial, on the
eternally unfinished unfolding choreography
of light and dark, and I crave radiance like air.

Act as Object

Response to Leah Hardy's sculpture "Listen"

listen : when activating
    the stasis
is the eye the ear?

If the act were object
it could shape itself so :

    hammered lily
that graphs the spinning phonemes :

    petal-flared pinna
fin   flipper   feather
  with hollowed calamus
to describe the lozenge
    of language :

      honeyed patina
of the auricle funneled
inward
channel to canal :

ear drum of the hollowed
    base   timpani
    of the boxed cochlear.

Here where sound
    is an invertebrate swirled
  in its metal shell :   shell
embroidered   with indentations
    and slender canines :

why not as well the voice
            box
    reverberating

sound flowing out
    that opened
  throat   the coppery
      furled lip?

If act were object   could we not hear :
    speak / listen as
  conjugations of a singular
        verb?

Regardez

They called me. I didn't choose them. —Philippe Petit

Those towers called to him while they were no more than an idea.
The girlfriend felt his hunger and twined her arms about his waist.
When he danced with the air, life hummed to him through the wire.
Apprenticed to a dream, their confidence was lyrical.

The girlfriend felt his hunger with her heart, and released him to it.
His boyhood friends, mesmerized by the perfection of his hope,
were so long apprenticed to the dream they felt only confidence.
They did not yet see how friends can be betrayed in such ascension.

The boyhood friends, content in the perfection of his hope,
trespassed with him, climbing, laden, to the anchor points.
Only later would they see betrayal in such ascension.
Now, tarped, they nest in the snarl of gear and each other.

Silent, frozen, the intruders rehearse the anchor points.
The night watchmen, unable to see the unexpected,
miss them nested in the snarl of gear and each other.
As the sun sets, darkness absorbs the hidden.

The night watchmen are unable to see the unlooked for.
The waiting men would never know another man like that.
The sun set and darkness absorbed the hidden, then
tarp peeled back like breaking membrane; the motionless arose.

The waiting men would never know another man like that.
Sleek the arrow, fine the filament that would trace the first line.
Once the tarp peeled back like broken membrane, the motionless arose.
Thread, cord, rope, cable, they pulled desire in hand over hand.

The dark arrow flew its fine line to the far tower's lip.
It became part of the conversation South had with North.
Thread, cord, rope, cable, he pulled desire in hand over hand.
Dawn finds them snugged, guyed, ready. How could he not hesitate?

But the wire calls over his hesitation, and he steps out.
Who doesn't want to defy the rules he flaunted?
He becomes part of the conversation South has with North.
Winged with his balance pole, the dark figure shimmers.

Who doesn't want to defy the rules he flaunted?
Even the policemen used the word "dance"
as winged with his balance pole, the dark figure shimmered.
Aloft, alone, he gestures his benediction to the crowd.

Even the policemen used the word "dance"
but they clipped him in cuffs and hustled him down.
Onlookers had felt the benediction of his gesture;
now the psychiatrist pronounced him sane but thirsty.

Police clipped his wings in cuffs and hustled him down
but how could a jail hold one whom gravity had not?
The psychiatrist pronounced him sane, only very thirsty.
The girl from the crowd on the station steps was so beautiful.

How could anything hold one whom gravity had not?
Oh, their bodies together seemed one with the pleasure.
The girl from the crowd on the station steps was so beautiful.
Now he knew what his flesh, and his breath, and his hunger were for.

His body, her body seemed at one with all pleasures.
When he danced with the air, life hummed to him through the wire.
Now he knew what his flesh, and his breath, and his hunger were for.
Those towers called to him while they were no more than an idea.

Grace

for Allan Eller

If you're lucky, at some point
ordinary life becomes itself:
something to inhabit, rather than
something to pass through. It's unserious
to express so banal an idea in these
postmodern times but it's all that he
could think of in the year it took for him
to die, that friend whose stay in ICU
turned out so much worse than had my own.

Early on I'd tried to encourage him
with that: how I'd lain in this very bed
and gotten my life back whole, a
futile hope, as it turned out, for him,
whose mind was clear to the end but
who remained locked into a body frozen
from the shoulders down. All that
apparatus of the respiratory system:
the weakened bellows of the lungs,
the compromised diaphragm, insufficient
in the end. Nothing about that contest
was ironic. Which reminds me

I should have the courage to say
cherish to describe the cove
of warmth, the hive our two bodies make
beneath the blankets, and the cooler
nimbus of the bedroom air around that hive.
The house's outer walls groan in the clench
of midnight cold while the glass
integument of windows blooms
with feathered frost, crystalline bargello
through which the silver winter moonlight
pours, yes,

I will let these hosannas out:
this baptismal of pearlescent light,
the eucharist of yet another
night nested together:
it is a grace, praise be,
it is our blessing to behold.

The Mare that You Loved

What She Didn't Seem to Know:

The last desperate procedure severed
all nerves to that foot months ago,
so her focus was the scent of spring
grass sweet in her nostrils,
wholly unconcerned
with her awkward step, the hoof flopping
aside, and her weight
pressed directly on bone, the inevitable
close now.

What She Did Seem to Know:

Moments after the needle slipped
back out of her neck, the panicked
cartwheeling, thrashing
her bewildered
eye fixed
on you, who had broken
the silver caul as she swam
fish-fetus from the womb,
you she had trusted all twenty
years of her life, you
who led her here to this place.

What You Can Only Hope She Knew:

The ragged hum of your voice
in her ear, the torn
stroke of your final
caress.

Time is a Horse

On the bus in Wales I happen
to be the one traveling through
on holiday, not the one in the midst
of her shopping, his business deal, the woman
staring steadfastly out the window, on her way
to the oncologist. Today, I am not the one
dying, though time is a horse, a runaway
none of us can dismount and so
the need is to find a way to enjoy the wind
that snatches handfuls of your hair as you race,
the horse's mane, your mane, the rhythm
and energy of the haunches powering under you,
their easy determination
to go on running.

Seawall

My first trip to Mount Desert Island was the summer
I turned twenty, four Augusts after the August
my mother died. A camping trip with the friend
who would one day become my sister-in-law.
Our first day on the island we picked up
a hitchhiker, young guy from Bleecker Street
in the Village, visiting Acadia as we were.
Caution tells us we should never have
opened ourselves to him like that—how impossible
it is now to explain the generational trust we felt then,
what we read in one another's clothes and hair.
The woman I would know for the rest of my life
and the young man we would never see again
roamed the park, contentedly, platonically,
while he took a veteran's pleasure in showing us
where the sweetest blueberries clung
to their granite escarpment, where the mudflats
plump with quahogs were. None of us seemed
to know the skies well enough to have heard
of the Perseids, but he knew Seawall and on our last
night there we carried blankets out to muffle
the stony beach, and lay down in the dark, rocked
by the lapping of the unseen waves, easy together
beneath the shower of frolicking stars.

High Summer

As suddenly tall
and lanky
as adolescents, the corn
stalks sprout
punk hairdos of pollened
tassels,
sex, sex, sex
is everywhere
on their brains as they lean
provocatively into
one another,
the green, folded
pockets
of their ears coyly
tucked among
fronds, that tremulous
silk.
The sun and their
own lithe bodies
tell them summer
is surely endless,
the high blue
sky collaborates
as if it too were steadfast.

Love Song

Sometimes,
pulled from dreaming
by the sudden absence in the bed
as you rise in early light,
I watch the figure padding from the room
with a shock of un-recognition
that is

delicious:
in my mouth, the taste
of my own reluctance
to return to the net
of consequences.

For the sheerest
instant

I strain
to hover:

      fish
twisting silver
 in the air

Hot August Night, 1978

Waiting for sleep I rest
my hands against the fruit
my womb would soon bear,
hands cupped around the succulent
pear-ness of that taut abdomen,
exploring the alien geography
of that bulge with no softness in it,
pronounced and confident as a bicep.

A coldness to contemplate
that strapping thug of a muscle.
Quiet in the summer dark I feel
the thrump of a foot, or an elbow,
stroking from within, the small swimmer
and I each in our way practicing
resignation, practicing what
it will feel like to let go.

First Suite

1. First Born

Last of August and she struggles into her separateness, muscle of unsayable needs and hungers, the natural fact that wails in the darkness and bites the breast that feeds her. In the miasma we rock her and she tutors us in all our basest appetites: now, and more, and deep.

2. First Bath

It's hard not to envy her unguarded acceptance of the body she has
not yet figured out is her own, *own* and *her* not being concepts she
has grasped as yet. She slips into the familiar buoyancy and warmth
of water, wholly at home in its element, content with the facilities
of limbs and digits and orifices. Even the labial lily of sex is on the
surface, easy. From her water-color eyes, she watches, considering,
as if she believes she could go back at any time, or choose to stay.

3. First Dance

She partners first with the Doberman, quadruped as she herself
has been until that point, and exactly the stature to support her
escape from gravity. She's got the dog by the neck, exuberant. The
Doberman recognizes they have discovered the meaning of life.
Together they set out for the uncharted world.

Second Born

He develops his own lop-sided crawl
on hands, knee, and a turbo-boost
from the other foot. Before long

he's teaching his father to fly.
My beat you down, he says
from the barn loft. Still lengths

ahead of Dad he sails under
the banister far above his line
of sight and runs out into air

like a cartoon character.
How surprising the world is,
he thinks on the flight down.

Hickory Down

1.

She slumped to the ground so quietly neither
of us heard her lie down above the big band
exuberance of that wind: exhausted dancer,

rested now in the grass with the ball gown
of her canopy crushed and billowing around her.

Hovering beside her, her partner of some sixty years
gnashes his branches, frets his leaves.

2.

Six weeks into her recumbency, the gray-green
leaves of the upended hickory sallow, only
an occasional fistful of branches rusting
to brown. The rest maintain a strained semblance
of themselves, drawing no doubt long stored energy
from the trunk, until October advances when,
like light that travels to us from a far-off, collapsed
star, those leaves golden into one final autumn.

3.

Our son calls the silhouettes of the twin
hickories on the ridge above the house,
part of the horizon line of his imagination,

what we'd all, without thinking about it,
grown to expect *home* to look like.
To others the serene hillside with its sentinel

hickory has no reason not to appear complete;
but to us the scene vibrates with the phantom
presence, that palpable energy of loss.

Waiting Out the Operation

I wish it were me instead...
We say those things about the suffering
of people we love but
it's vapory hyperbole:
our own mortal bodies
are glad in their every molecule
that it is not them

All of the hours his mother lies
on an operating table my husband
goes about the tasks
of his everyday life repulsed
by the ordinariness
of which he is capable:

he whistles the horses in
from their misty pastures
and portions out their breakfast grain;
his awkward overshoes
leave darkened prints
in the silver of the dewy grass.

At lunch my husband sighs, he slams
the mayonnaise jar on the counter
but layers on the meat and washes
the sandwich down with ice water.

How lovely, I think,
is the anguish it causes him
to be glad.

Backing a Colt for the First Time

It's exactly the fact that you could die
that lets you forget you will die.

As separate now from the muck
of the everyday as you are from the ground,
even the mortgage, your son's
calculus grade, or your husband's mother
ebbing away in her hospital bed

replaced by instinct,
rhythm and sinew,
by unpredictability
and the quickness beneath you.

This suspension
in danger and pleasure is bodily,
pure
and compellingly whole.

Embrace

What we cannot
let go of the hope of
is that words can somehow be found
to describe
in that pure sense   of   de-scribe :

to write so accurately around
that absence becomes   immanent

Give in to what the body knows :

touch is our only eloquence

Anniversary

for my father

Jews call it *yarhtzeit,*
the Bangladeshi *shraadh.*
Intent as we are with
getting over, getting on,
Americans have no term.

October again, and the trees
make such a pageantry of loss:
orpiment, vermilion, cadmium leaves
quiver in the steel wind
that bites them free.

In the long remembering of trees
you are nearly there
where you are not, and have not
been some nine years now.

I am at home here
in the cascade
of their radiant perishing.

Jack

Years have passed since I last entered
a church to be a part of those rituals
of chant, vestment, statuary, and incense
from which I am also descended, yet
October ends and I find myself

elbow-deep in a vegetable once again,
scooping out the skull of a jack-o'-lantern
hands slicked with the vivid mess, acolyte
to the animate knife, eager for that lurid face
blazing its eyes against the long, deep dark.

Felt like a Thought

No verge only merge:
inebriate on November sun
the golden cats embrace and rollick
in the golden leaf litter, the press
of their thick-pelted, muscular
bodies voices the maple leaves'
crisp song crinkling beneath them,
the lick of the grass's innumerable
cool tongues, the excitation of the wind,
the tumult of geese chevrons
clamorously rowing the skies overhead:
this singular instant of a singular
afternoon plump as ripened fruit:
how few autumns cats have:
how completely they have them.

Want

The corn field's somnolent
summer idyll is ended.
Over slow months of sinuous
emergence, the brute
April day of mechanical
seeding had been forgotten,
likewise that quarter-grown
May day the tractor swept
a crystalline shower of chemicals
overhead to douse and shrivel
the broad leaf competition. Since then,
only the delicate unfolding, rooting,
reaching, synthesizing the sun
to green rustle, and the occasional
small foray of masked raccoons,
the furtive penetration of deer, or the
intermittent, self-possessed wallow
of bear, but now, in autumn, we've
hollowed out, desiccated
to a tawny susurration of reedy
voices, and above that
murmuring the unmistakable
clack and rumble:
the harvester, in its relentless
confidence, arrives.

We have always known you wanted us.

On the Ground in Philadelphia

The pilot's voice
has the timbre of regret   sorry
about this, folks   failure   emergency
federal law insists   ailerons   have had to declare
landing
on the ground emergency
vehicles   very fast   no
real
worry   we'll
talk to you
again   when we're on the ground   follow
the flight attendant's
directions

What will you do with the twenty minutes left in your life?

strapped to your seat
emptied
grim   rehearsing nothing
but the route to the hatch two rows back

and the video you once   twice
watched from your armchair

Sioux City, Iowa   DC10 in incandescent
cartwheels
opening to bright pieces

The black and buoyant
night beyond
that small window

                        too far off
           to care about   the lights
       of Philadelphia
       rushing
           up to you   nothing
                   you need to see

       and then we are suspended
                       inside the hurtling
       the keening of the brakes the lurid
       alarm lights licking   the indifferent shriek
   of air rushing along the plane's
           frail skin   de-
                   creasing   de
               creasing
                       de

       and we are applauding
               clapping together hands that hold
       the life we have been returned to

           ambulances and fire trucks with their
               jocular lights   wink beside us

           as we roll home
                       plucked
           from that far place.

The Geometry of Grief

Beneath the canopy sheltering
the open rectangle from which
there is no shelter, mourners huddle

connecting and enclosing the circles
of their loss, while out beyond
the line of the cemetery fence,

the undertaker's assistant
slouches in his black suit,
discreetly shooting the breeze

with the grave diggers who lean
and wait, their yellow-slickered pants
mud-spattered and gay.

Time enough and space
for grief to find them too
but today, the rain surrounding them

is April's, silver and sweet.
The grass just greening at their feet
feathers the ground like a promise.

The Wedding Tent

opens an envelope of light, a paper lantern of exaltation
in the perfect dark of the evening field. Here the rabbit,

deer, the skunk, and fox, mouse, mole and vole,
all the habitués of that nocturnal space hold back

from the high-spirited human dishevelment
of dance and laughter and song. Beside this cell

of celebration the bonfire blazes its approval
in an incandescent spray of extinguishing stars.

for Lizzy & Sebastian

Love Among the Long-married

The long-married shop
for a new mattress, king-sized,
luxuriant as the beds in nice hotels
where they'd now and then had
a special evening. It's been
twenty years since their last
new mattress. The long-married
do the math and realize
they may never wear this new one out…

***

For their thirty-fifth wedding anniversary,
the long-married plant a tree.

Yes, they are exactly
that stubborn.

***

The long-married tell one another:
Our memories are not what they used to be
but in memory

we *are who we used to be:*

your touch
your touch alone

and we slip slick
into our 26 year-old bodies
young   electric   and sleek

no one else
no one else
can offer that

***

The long-married visit the aquarium:
hand-in-hand in the tunnel-tank where
    the cold, blank-eyed
        shapes of sharks drift by,
   drift around them
serene
    and confident.

Curing

Thirty-four years after we built the house, we're adding
on the mudroom we wanted but could not afford then,
an extravagance we hope to live long enough to justify.

Peering into the hole nipped into the yard beside the kitchen door
at the freshly-poured foundation curing, I feel the phantom
of an infant in my arms, a memory the weight and size

of our firstborn whom I held that thirty-four-year-ago twilight
when we drove up the gash of the newly-cut driveway to view
the maw just opened for the basement of this very house.

On the crest of the excavated dirt that night a disoriented vixen
trotted, sniffed and stared, sniffed and stared, her home having clearly
been displaced for ours. One backward glare and she melted

into the woods. Of course the infant I held then has babies
of her own now. These days I stand in the past even when I am
most present, most in the present, my memories the element

through which I experience experience. Is this richness?
or rigidity? What I know is each morning of this summer
when I pull from my bed, easing my joints from sleep into

the day, through the window I can see Anastasia and Virginia
with their fillies, grazing in the pasture just beyond the green
and burgeoning garden, those two fillies our future, our last

generation in a life's work, yes, even the future begins now
to feel final, and I find myself suffused with recognition
of the blessing it is to have reached such a shore.

Anniversary in Paris

We were never young in Paris as the lovers on le Pont de l'Archevêché
are now, initialling their padlock and squeezing it into the bristle

and glitter of the others. They kiss and toss the key to the Seine.
Forty years into our marriage we know better than to think of love

as a lock, but we wish them well. In their version of this day
we are the aging couple on the park bench behind Notre Dame,

part of the furniture of the world giving witness to the theater
of their lives, but in our version, they are familiars of our animate past,

the unfaded memory of our youth's garden, and now the brides arrive,
the extravagent froth of their dresses bunched up into their arms

and spilling over into the arms of their attentive grooms, couples fused
by their efforts to bear her dress up above the soil until they reach

the bridge, where the trailing photographer settles them against
the lock-festooned railing, with the silvered Seine and the elegant

bulk of Notre Dame a frame behind them. With no camera trained
on us we find ourselves nevertheless lofted as if the momentary

gift of the image's suspension in time were our own : the embrace
of bride and groom on the bridge beneath the sail of the wafted bridal veil.

A Serious House

A serious house on serious earth it is,
In whose blent air all our compulsions meet,
Are recognized, and robed as destinies.
And that much can never be obsolete.

　　　　　　　　　　　　　　　　—Philip Larkin

I. Chartres Cathedral

Driving towards Chartres
from the east the cathedral
even today floats above the fields
like a dream of the everlasting.

From any point in the city
weave up the cobbled streets
climbing to God, or at the least,
to a collective dream of the divine
worked out in stone and shards
of jeweled glass.

How to suggest the refreshment
and drama this space was
to its builders, living lives that
would seem to us brief and brute ?
How other-worldly...

Outside the flying buttresses,
lithe as stone dancers in repose,
lean against the walls,
easeful over centuries.

Inside the air is numinous:
light falls unfathomable
stories, like the still
irradiating glow
that travels to us
from extinguished stars.

II. Mont Saint-Michel

Enisled on its rock, pooled
in the palm of sea and sky
like a poem on its page :

exposed, and sheltered.
Shaped in necessary
harmony with the bedrock,
choired by wind and gulls.

Cloister, fortress, prison,
sanctuary : consecrated first
October 16, 709,
over ground Celts had
already dedicated
to the underworld.

Seven oh nine.
That first oratory built
at the insistence, it is said,
of the archangel Michael
who badgered a reluctant
St. Aubert, the irrepressible
necessity of the project at last
impressed upon the bishop
when the angel burnt a hole
in Aubert's skull
with a heavenly finger.

Chapel to church to cathedral;
monks and pilgrims to knights,
scriptorium refurbished as salle de chevalier;
besieged for thirty years but unconquered;
repurposed as a prison by the Revolution,
the first inmates clerics who refused

to abjure their vows. At last, in 1836,
voices like that of Victor Hugo
reclaimed the site as heritage.

Today even the daytime crush
of tourists cannot overpower
the palpable presences—
one could never feel alone here–
but as day fades from the leadlight
windows and night begins to settle
over the rock, petitioners' candles
gutter out in the sanctuary of St. Pierre,
the parish church at the abbey's base,
and in the abbey's nave the medieval
Madonna rests her Holy Child
upon her knee: the insistent penetration
of her gaze softens in the gloaming.

III. Sainte-Chappelle

Liquid with light
Sainte-Chappelle is a
reliquary of effervescent

ambition   a buoyant
repository of piety and power
elemental in the most

ethereal sense   stone
mortar mineral and glass
transubstantiated to weightlessness

incorporeal
stone made celestial
alchemy nearly

powerful enough
to provoke faith in
all it was formed to praise

IV. Notre Dame, Île de la Cité, Paris

Notre Dame is collectivity and the individual soul
wrought in limestone and handmade glass.

This is a building only aggregate effort, mass
industry over generations, could possibly have
achieved, while the individual figures
of the friezes, the gargling gargoyles
animated from stone each shaped by the singular,

such a mob of sculptures, some positioned where
the maker would have had to have believed
only God would ever see, each chiseled
and polished with the devotion that audience
of one inspired, a prayer in stone.

Have the old narratives the windows
depict worn out?   that public god
of incense, pews and ritual ?

In the altered, vaulted light
of this shaped space
feel the god of otherness and awe
        undiminished

To-Do List for the Final Decades

Fall in love in a foreign language.

Compose a navigation song to chart your losses,
and the way back.

Learn to skate on the skin, the inexpressibly thin
membrane where water meets the air:
master the skill of carving a caress
into that tensile surface, a calligraphy
as tender as hope.

Hold out your hand for mercy, that unlikely
muscle of a bird which must
row its wings, or plummet.

Follow the silver river to its source, alone
in the underbrush of origins, at the last
on hands and knees, torn and pulling
towards the heart, the one moist
pulse, obeying.

Formulate a new conception of heaven.
No need to bother with hell which we
reinvent over and over again without ceasing.

Dance the slip jig in Lettermore,
the gavotte in Brittany; succumb
to the merengue, the mambo, the salsa;
hoof it with the donkey man in Barbados.

Plant a moon garden of pearl-petalled blossoms:
voluptuous, excessive as the baroque: peony,
clematis, ranunculus and damask rose warming the darkness.
Collaborate with birds in an anti-anthem
that will un-snarl the drums and pacify the pipes.
Let the meadowlark teach the wren, the thrush tutor

the bunting, let the pipit pass the melody to the bulbul,
let their song enter human bodies like scent,
scent that will conjure up sunlight, their mother's
lap, their own father's strong, young laughter.

Hybridize happiness: graft
the tree of the Knowledge of Good
and Evil to the Roots of Despair. Fertilize generously.
Devour a pomegranate, a persimmon, saskatoon,
guava, kumquat, honeyberry, quince, papaya,
loganberry, elderberry, cherimoya, hautbois,
all fruits sacred and profane. Let the juices
bless your fingers, anoint your breast.

Accommodate your own prodigal idealism: kill
the fatted calf for truth; strike
the timbrel, sing in the purpled
shadows of dusk now, sing.

Wave farewell with the torn
scarf of your heart.
Welcome into yourself the evening's holy silence.

Trick Rider

His handsprings and gesticulations are a semaphore of well-phrased questions. The hinge of his bent knees absorbs the shock. The daring Trick Rider has an abiding faith in three-four time. Teetering on the rump of the world, he trusts what his feet know. Clinging to the belly of the world, Trick Rider feels the enormity of the heart beating against his own, he senses the menace and the excitation of hooves stroking that thin amnion of air along his back. Trick Rider hears the audience roar as the fetus hears the father's voice. Now he's streaming off the side of the world like a flag. Vision is a ribbon of fluid color, thought an arc in the back. Sweat-streaked, unrepentant, he stands on top of the world, wreathed in a vapor of dust.